THE WOMEN OF THE BIBLE
Speak

WORKBOOK

*The Wisdom of 16 Women and
Their Lessons for Today*

SHANNON BREAM

HarperChristian
Resources

The Women of the Bible Speak Workbook

© 2022 by Fox News Network LLC

Requests for information should be addressed to:

HarperChristian Resources, 3900 Sparks Dr. SE, Grand Rapids, Michigan 49546

ISBN 978–0–310–15595-9 (softcover)

ISBN 978–0–310–15596-6 (ebook)

HarperChristian Resources titles may be purchased in bulk for church, business, fundraising, or ministry use. For information, please e-mail ResourceSpecialist@ChurchSource.com.

Fox News Book imprint and logo are trademarks of Fox News Network LLC.

First Printing September 2022 / Printed in the United States of America

Contents

Welcome

Women are central to some of the most critical events, powerful encounters, and transformative moments in the Bible. They change the course of history.

In the upcoming pages, you'll explore the stories of sixteen women and dig deep into their lives. You'll find that these aren't just characters from an ancient book. These are real people who lived and breathed and hoped and prayed. They cried and celebrated just like you.

They offered themselves as voices of truth and reason. They stepped boldly into impossible situations and played critical roles in saving countless lives and even nations.

We must remember that these aren't fictional superheroes. They faced challenges much like the ones we face today: the pangs of loneliness, the sting of rejection, and the quiet ache of the soul. They, too, battled the disappointment and depression that comes with unfulfilled expectations and personal loss. Yet these extraordinary women rose above because God was their refuge.

In Him, they found hope and healing.

In Him, they found power and provision.

In Him, they found strength and sustenance.

And the same God who worked mightily in their lives is at work in yours, too. May you find comfort and hope as we make this journey together.

* * *

How to Use
This Workbook

This workbook is a companion to the #1 *New York Times* bestselling book, *The Women of the Bible Speak* by Shannon Bream, and it's designed to make your experience richer and deeper. In the upcoming sixteen lessons, you'll be challenged to consider the parallels between each woman's story and your own. You'll be asked to reflect on how God worked in their lives and how He's working in your own.

If you join with friends or neighbors to complete this workbook, consider answering the questions personally *before* you meet up. That way you'll be the most prepared with insights, reflections, and thoughts to share.

You'll notice that each lesson has four components:

REFLECT invites you to read key moments of each woman's life in the Bible and connect with their stories.

CONNECT asks you to consider how God in the Old Testament or Jesus in the New Testament responds to each woman and what this discloses about His character and how He responds to you.

REVEAL provides an opportunity to identify specific character traits, responses to God, and acts of faith, as well as your similar traits, responses, and acts of faith.

PRAY asks you to prayerfully consider how the woman's story ties into the work God is doing in your life right now.

Every other lesson features a bonus section:

PAIRS reveals that individually, every woman's story is powerful. Here, you'll consider the women in pairs, finding the commonalities in their callings and challenges. Some of the women knew one another. Others were connected simply by a thread of common purpose, one that becomes clearer by studying the women side by side.

SARAH

The facts of Sarah's life sound like an adventure story, full of twists and turns: She was settled into her life when her husband suddenly announced they'd be upending everything they knew to move way out of their comfort zone. She managed a wealthy household with a very complicated blended family—and that's not all. She bore no child of her own, and even when God made her a specific promise, she laughed it off as impossible. How surprised she must have been when the wildly unthinkable finally came true for her—but oh, how far off track she'd already gotten by taking matters into her own hands.

—From *The Women of the Bible Speak*, page 1

*I*n looking at women of the Bible, it's easy to think we'll find stunning portraits of perfection, flawless creatures of valor. More often, we find people—just like us—with strengths and weaknesses, people who can make great sacrifices and yet exhibit great selfishness.

Sarah, the wife of Abraham, demonstrates that despite our flaws, we can be used by our Heavenly Father to weave together His highest purposes. Sarah is the perfect illustration of this beautiful, complex truth.

REFLECT

One of the most important details to pay attention to when studying the Bible is the first moment a person is introduced. This often reveals something profound or insightful about the person's story or character.

Read Genesis 11:27–32. What details about Sarah's life are revealed at her introduction? (Hint: v. 29–30) Why is this important to know early on?

If you were being introduced in the Bible, what detail about your life would be listed first?

Read Genesis 12:1, 4–6. What does God call Abraham to do?

What impact did this have on Sarah?

If you were Sarah, how would you have responded?

Which of the following best describes how you would feel? (Circle) each that apply.

Excited	Angry	Joyful	Confused	Anxious	Hopeful
Fearful	Irked	Sorrowful	Leery	Eager	Worried

Which of the following best describes Sarah's response? (Circle) each that apply.

Cooperative	Whiny	Brave	Willing	Surprised

God's call for Abraham and Sarah to leave everything is also accompanied by powerful promises.

Read Genesis 12:2–3 and Genesis 17:15 and fill in the chart below.

Details of God's Promise to Abraham	Details of God's Promise to Sarah

What do the promises have in common? How do they differ?

What stands out to you about God's promise to Sarah?

Though Abraham and Sarah are a power couple, they also share deep flaws and weaknesses. Both are sometimes fearful and tempted to take matters into their own hands.

Read Genesis 12:9–20. How do you think Sarah felt being placed in potential danger because of Abraham's decision to lie?

How did God protect Sarah? (Hint: v. 17)

Read Genesis 20:1–18. How do you think Sarah felt being placed in potential danger because of Abraham's decision to lie again?

How did God protect Sarah? (Hint: v. 3)

What do these two parallel stories reveal about the following:

* The character of Abraham:

* The character of Sarah:

* The character of God:

Sarah remains voiceless until chapter 16 of Genesis when, for the first time, she has something to say, and it's a gamechanger.

Read Genesis 16:1–6. How does Sarah respond to her infertility?

What situation in your life are you most tempted to take control of rather than trust God?

> *F*ollowing ancient Near Eastern custom, Sarah hatched a plan to produce an heir: sending Abraham to "go into [her] maid," Hagar, so she could "obtain children through her." But as sometimes happens when we stop trusting God's plan and go our own way, things went terribly wrong.
>
> —From *The Women of the Bible Speak*, page 4

Read Genesis 17:15–19 and Genesis 18:1–15. How does Abraham respond to the promise of a child?

How does Sarah respond to the promise of a child?

What compels Sarah to lie (v. 15)?

Describe a recent situation that tempted or caused you to lie. What motivated you to not tell the truth?

Read Genesis 21:1–7. How does Sarah respond to the miraculous birth?

What has been your biggest joy come true?

The Bible tells us that Sarah "dealt harshly" with Hagar (Genesis 16:6). It's the same wording the Bible uses for the way the Egyptians treat their Jewish slaves in Exodus, meaning with oppression and forced labor. Abraham gave Sarah complete authority over Hagar, knowing what it would mean for the servant woman, and he stood by while Sarah abused the pregnant woman with impunity.

—From *The Women of the Bible Speak*, page 5

Read Genesis 21:8–21. What does Sarah's refusal to use the name of her servant or her servant's child suggest about Sarah's attitude toward them?

Did Sarah go too far this time in asking Abraham to end his relationship with his eldest son, to send him away so that he may never see him again? Why or why not?

We do not hear Sarah's voice again, though other voices in Scripture refer to her. Yet she's mentioned and heralded in the New Testament because God worked through her.

Read Hebrews 11:11 and 1 Peter 3:5–6. What do these passages commend Sarah for doing?

CONNECT

Now that you've read and reflected on much of Sarah's story and various mentions of her throughout the Bible, it's time to connect this woman of the Bible with your own life. Fill out the chart below.

What do you see as Sarah's greatest character strengths?	
What do you see as Sarah's greatest character weaknesses?	
Which strengths do you relate to or long for?	
Which weaknesses do you relate to or long to overcome?	
How do you hope to be more like Sarah in your faith journey?	

$\mathscr{R}$EVEAL

Now that you've connected this woman of the Bible with your own life, it's time to look at how God reveals His character and faithfulness to Sarah and how God does the same for you.

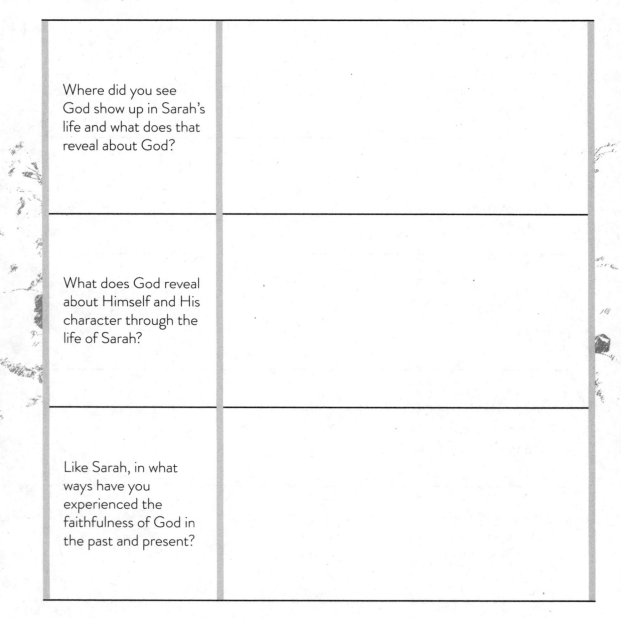

Where did you see God show up in Sarah's life and what does that reveal about God?	
What does God reveal about Himself and His character through the life of Sarah?	
Like Sarah, in what ways have you experienced the faithfulness of God in the past and present?	

$\mathcal{P}$RAY

Take a few minutes to ask the Holy Spirit to guide you as you respond to the following prayer prompts.

Lord, like Sarah, help me . . .

_____

_____

_____

Lord, toward whom am I being harsh and hard-hearted? How can I show Your kindness and love toward those people?

_____

_____

_____

Lord, where am I most tempted to take matters into my own hands? How can I trust You more?

_____

_____

_____

Lord, considering Sarah's story, how are You calling me to live differently?

_____

_____

_____

HAGAR

H agar was a person, a vulnerable woman without any real protectors in the world, an enslaved woman who was never given any choices, a mother who wanted life and happiness for her son. If we can separate Hagar from the layers of symbolism heaped on her by later generations, we can recover some sense of who she was and what she might have to say to us today.

—From *The Women of the Bible Speak*, page 16

Of all the women we're studying, Hagar is the only one who's the property of her owner. While she's identified as a trusted servant of Sarah in Genesis 16, as her story progresses, the language reveals that Hagar was seen and treated as a slave.

It's hard to read Hagar's story without feeling compassion. She experienced great unfairness throughout life. Yet Hagar reminds us that there's no place we can go where God's eyes are not on us.

ℛEFLECT

In antiquity, fertility was incredibly significant in the ways you saw yourself and how others viewed you. Giving birth provided women a way to gain status and security. For Abraham and Sarah, the birth of a son would fulfill God's promises.

Read Genesis 16:1–3. What decisions do Sarah and Abraham make in this passage?

What decisions is Hagar permitted to make in this passage?

Describe a time when decisions were made for you. How did you feel? Respond? Act?

Read Genesis 16:4–6. How does Sarah treat Hagar?

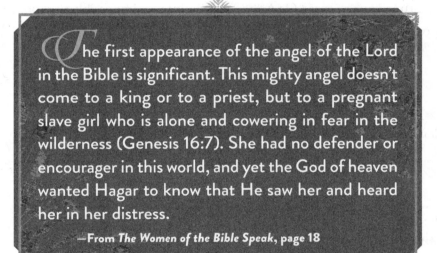

The first appearance of the angel of the Lord in the Bible is significant. This mighty angel doesn't come to a king or to a priest, but to a pregnant slave girl who is alone and cowering in fear in the wilderness (Genesis 16:7). She had no defender or encourager in this world, and yet the God of heaven wanted Hagar to know that He saw her and heard her in her distress.

—From *The Women of the Bible Speak*, page 18

Read Genesis 16:7–9. What surprises you most about how God responds to Hagar?

What does God's response reveal about His character?

What does the angel of the Lord instruct Sarah to do in verse 9?

On a scale of one to ten, how hard do you think it was for Hagar to hear and obey this?

Describe a time you've sensed God nudging you into an impossible situation. How did you respond?

Read Genesis 16:10–12. What's most comforting in what the angel told Hagar?

What's the hardest thing the angel told Hagar?

How would you have responded?

Hagar then becomes the first person in the Bible to give God a name: "El Roi," which means, literally, "the God who sees me." God had seen her perfectly the whole time, and now she had seen God.

Read Genesis 16:13–16. Why was it so important that Hagar felt seen by God?

Where do you feel most invisible to God?

In Genesis 21, the long-awaited promise is fulfilled when Sarah conceives and gives birth to Isaac. Yet rather than grow tender, Sarah's heart becomes harder toward Hagar.

Read Genesis 21:9–11. Which of the following best describes Sarah's attitude and response to Hagar? Circle all that apply.

Which of the following best describe Abraham's attitude and response to Sarah? Underline all that apply.

Cruel	Selfish	Jealous	Patient	Hard-hearted
Excited	Angry	Apologetic	Fearful	Distressed
Harsh	Cold	Shocked	Gracious	Other _____

What do you suspect fueled Sarah's response?

When have you wrestled with these same feelings and responses?

Read Genesis 21:12–21. Where do you see the faithfulness and kindness of God in this passage?

What does this reveal about how God speaks to you and what He does for you in your distress?

Where do you most need to be reminded of this now?

CONNECT

Now that you've read and reflected on much of Hagar's story and various mentions of her throughout the Bible, it's time to connect this woman of the Bible with your own life. Fill out the chart below.

What do you see as Hagar's greatest character strengths?	
What do you see as Hagar's greatest character weaknesses?	
Which strengths do you relate to or long for?	
Which weaknesses do you relate to or long to overcome?	
How do you hope to be more like Hagar in your faith journey?	

REVEAL

Now that you've connected this woman of the Bible with your own life, it's time to look at how God reveals His character and faithfulness to Hagar and how God is doing the same for you.

Where did you most see God show up in Hagar's life?	
What does God reveal about Himself and His character in the life of Hagar?	
Like Hagar, in what ways have you experienced God truly seeing you?	
What's the wilderness where God most wants to meet you and rescue you from now?	

$\mathcal{P}$RAY

Take a few minutes to ask the Holy Spirit to guide you as you respond to the following prayer prompts.

Lord, like Hagar, help me . . .

_____

_____

_____

Lord, how well do You really see me? How well do You really know me?

_____

_____

_____

Lord, show me where I'm feeling most out of control and how my responses are hurting others. Will You give me the compassion and kindness toward difficult people?

_____

_____

_____

Lord, show me where I'm hurting and feel most isolated and abandoned right now. I know You see me, but how are You going to meet me and lead me in this?

_____

_____

_____

$\mathcal{P}$AIRS

We often look at women in the Bible on their own. By looking at them in pairs according to their relationships and life situations, we can better understand ourselves, God, and others.

The Apostle Paul later contrasts Sarah and Hagar. In Galatians, he explains that these women represent two different covenants. Sarah and her son, Isaac, represent a covenant of freedom. Hagar and her son, Ishmael, represent a covenant of bondage. He leveraged this comparison to show how the Jewish law brought religious bondage. Though the law was good, it could never free people from the slavery of sin. Meanwhile the covenant of freedom, demonstrated through Sarah and Isaac, would eventually bring freedom in Christ.

Read Galatians 4:21–31. How does Paul use these women's stories as symbols for the work of Christ?

How have you experienced Sarah and Hagar as more than symbols and instead as real, living women through your study?

How might Hagar's and Sarah's stories be different if they had found a way to connect with each other, to forgive each other, to understand each other's grief?

With whom in your life do you have a Sarah-Hagar relationship?

What creative steps can you take to find connection with that person?

What would it look like for you to practice forgiveness, extend kindness, and understand the other person's pain?

What do you suspect could be the outcome of such generous compassion?

RACHEL

One of the stages of grief, counselors tell us, is bargaining. We say to God, okay, what do I have to do to undo this pain and get what I want? Seen this way, Rachel's life appears to be one long stage of grief, because she is constantly bargaining. She is always looking for a way to "fix" her situation, and in that she is very much like the man she married.

—**From** *The Women of the Bible Speak*, **page 32**

*R*achel provides us with one of the great romance and love stories of the ages. Much like Sarah whom we've studied, Rachel struggles with infertility, jealousy, rivalry, and taking matters into her own hands. Yet Rachel's story reminds us that despite our weaknesses and mistakes, our loving God still sees us, listens to us, and answers our prayers in amazing ways.

*R*EFLECT

After deceiving his father and taking his brother's birthright, Jacob is sent away. He has a powerful dream and encounter with God. Then he comes to a well, where he encounters a stunning woman who will change the course of his life.

Read Genesis 29:1–12. Write a description of Rachel based on this passage in the space below.

How does Jacob respond to Rachel? (Hint: v. 10–11)

Read Genesis 29:13–20. What are the differences between Rachel and her sister, Leah?

Whom do you relate to more: Rachel or Leah? Why?

Read Genesis 29:21–30. How does Laban deceive Jacob? (Hint: v. 23–25)

What do Laban's actions reveal about how he values his daughters?

Rachel remains barren and Leah gives birth to multiple children. This stirs jealousy and sparks a sharp rivalry. The two sisters get caught up in a fierce competition to see who can have the most children.

Read Genesis 30:1–21. What is Rachel's response to her sister and Jacob regarding her infertility? (Hint: v. 1)

How does Rachel take matters into her own hands like Sarah? (Hint: v. 3–5)

> ᴛragedy in the human realm isn't always the result of God's judgment, but it does always present an opportunity to show His glory. It's likely Rachel couldn't see that far ahead, feeling only that she was being judged by God and that her sentence of infertility was connected to God's favoring her sister. Rachel viewed it as a battle, and she wanted victory.
>
> —From *The Women of the Bible Speak*, page 34

In what ways do Rachel and Leah want what the other sister has been given?

In which relationships are you struggling with jealousy and rivalry now?

How is the jealousy and rivalry affecting you? The other person? Those around you?

How can you change your attitude and responses toward the person?

Read Genesis 30:22–24. What does God specifically do for Rachel?

Why do you think God listened to Rachel?

What does this reveal about God's character?

What does this reveal about the power of fervent prayer?

What role does prayer play in your everyday life?

What stops you from praying more?

From this moment, there's no more recorded struggle between Rachel and Leah. They live in harmony and unity even as they follow Jacob back to his homeland. Along the way, Jacob is reconciled with his brother, Esau, and Rachel becomes pregnant.

Read Genesis 35:16–20. What names do Rachel and Jacob give to their son?

How does Jacob honor Rachel by renaming their son?

What does this reveal about Jacob's lifelong love of Rachel?

What does it reveal about God that He would use a highly dysfunctional family, including Rachel and Leah, to give birth to the twelve tribes of Israel?

How does this give you hope that God can use anyone to accomplish His purposes?

CONNECT

Now that you've read and reflected on much of Rachel's story and various mentions of her throughout the Bible, it's time to connect this woman of the Bible with your own life. Fill out the chart below.

What do you see as Rachel's greatest character strengths?	
What do you see as Rachel's greatest character weaknesses?	
Which strengths do you relate to or long for?	
Which weaknesses do you relate to or long to overcome?	
How do you hope to be more fervent in prayer like Rachel in your faith journey?	

ℛEVEAL

Now that you've connected this woman of the Bible with your own life, it's time to look at how God reveals His character and goodness to Rachel and how God is doing the same for you.

Where did you most see God show up in Rachel's life?	
What does God reveal about Himself and His character through the life of Rachel?	
Like Rachel, in what ways have you experienced God listening to you?	
What is the prayer in your heart you most long for God to hear and respond to?	

$\mathscr{P}$RAY

Take a few minutes to ask the Holy Spirit to guide you as you respond to the following prayer prompts.

Lord, like Rachel, help me . . .

_____

_____

_____

Lord, where am I allowing rivalry and jealousy to get the best of me? How can I break free from my unhealthy attitudes and actions?

_____

_____

_____

Lord, where are You asking me to trust You more?

_____

_____

_____

Lord, considering Rachel's story, how are You calling me to pray more fervently?

_____

_____

_____

ℒEAH

That Jesus came to this world through Leah's off-spring is a wonderful picture: God waits for us not only in the places of beauty and popularity, but also often in the places of brokenness and rejection, the darkest valleys, and the ugliest messes. There we find God deeply present, seeing our misery and bringing us our most precious blessing, just as He did for His daughter, Leah.

—**From** *The Women of the Bible Speak*, **page 49**

Few people in the Bible play second fiddle to someone quite like Leah. The older sister of Rachel, Leah is introduced as someone constantly being compared to her sister. Rachel is physically stunning and lovely, Leah is not. Rachel is the dream wife of Jacob, Leah is not. Yet despite playing runner-up to her younger sister for much of her life, God enters Leah's pain and sadness and blesses and provides for her abundantly. Leah's story reminds us that when we feel most pushed down, God is ready to lift us up.

ℛEFLECT

As mentioned previously, a person's introduction in the Bible is always worth noting, because it often highlights significant features in the person's character and characteristics of their life.

Read Genesis 29:16–17. How do Leah and Rachel's descriptions differ?

What, if anything, do the descriptions of these women have in common?

Who is someone in your family, friendships, or life to whom you've been compared?

How did those comparisons affect you? The other person?

Read Genesis 29:18–30. How does Laban trick Jacob into marrying Leah?

Why would Laban have stooped to this kind of trickery?

How do think Laban's actions made Leah feel about the marriage? Her sister? Her self-worth?

Read Genesis 29:31–35. What does the Lord see about Leah's situation? (Hint: v. 31)

Where do you most feel unseen, unloved, or disliked now?

How does Leah's story give you hope?

Throughout Genesis, the mothers often name their children and those names often reveal the mother's spiritual state—think of Rachel naming her final child "Son of Pain," or Sarah commemorating her laughter in Isaac's name.

What does Leah say about each of her sons?

> Reuben:
>
> Simeon:
>
> Levi:
>
> Judah:

What do her statements about each son reveal about her spiritual growth and relationship with God?

In what area of your life do you feel unloved, invisible, or less than?

Like Leah, have you been able to praise God in those circumstances? Why or why not?

When Rachel sees the four sons of Leah, she turns to her maid, Bilhah, to create children with Jacob. Bilhah gives birth to two sons, and Leah copycats the strategy.

Read Genesis 30:1–13. What does Leah say about her two sons?

Gad:

Asher:

What do Leah's statements reveal about her spiritual growth and relationship with God?

How has Leah found faith and joy outside of her difficult circumstances?

Where do you most need to find faith and joy outside of your difficult circumstances?

Though Leah may not ever have received her husband's love, she most certainly received God's blessing. Through her son Levi came Moses, Aaron, Miriam, and all the priests of Israel. Her son Judah became a great prince and gave his name not only to the entire southern half of the kingdom of Israel, Judea, but also to the People of the Book, the Jews. Judah was also the ancestor of King David.

Leah probably dreamed of an escape from the never-ending contest with her sister, but without that relationship, Leah may never have grown into a calm, confident woman of God.

—From *The Women of the Bible Speak*, page 48

When have you thought, *My life would be so much easier without this irritating person in it?*

How did that person cause you to grow and trust in God more?

How does Leah's story demonstrate that God isn't just found in popularity and outward beauty, but also in brokenness and difficulties?

CONNECT

Now that you've read and reflected on much of Leah's story, it's time to connect this woman of the Bible with your life. Fill out the chart below.

What do you see as Leah's greatest character strengths?	
What do you see as Leah's greatest character weaknesses?	
Which strengths do you relate to or long for?	
Which weaknesses do you relate to or long to overcome?	
How do you hope to be more like Leah in your faith journey?	

REVEAL

Now that you've connected with this woman of the Bible, it's time to look at how God reveals His character and faithfulness to Leah and how God is doing the same for you.

Where did you most see God show up in Leah's life and what does that reveal about God?	
What does God reveal about Himself and His character in the life of Leah?	
Like Leah, in what ways do you grow through disappointment and difficult circumstances?	
How is God revealing Himself to you right now?	

$\mathscr{P}$RAY

Take a few minutes to ask the Holy Spirit to guide you as you respond to the following prayer prompts.

Lord, like Leah, help me . . .

_____

_____

_____

Lord, with whom have I fallen into the comparison trap? How can I celebrate the work You're doing in my life and praise You?

_____

_____

_____

Lord, where am I clinging to pain and disappointment? How can I grow in trust of Your redeeming work?

_____

_____

_____

Lord, who is someone I find irritating whom You're using to shape me into the image of Christ? How can I embrace that person and Your work more?

_____

_____

_____

Lord, considering Leah's story, how are You calling me to live differently?

_____

_____

_____

$\mathcal{P}$ A I R S

We often look at women in the Bible on their own. By looking at them in pairs, according to their relationships and life situations, we can better understand ourselves, God, and others.

At Bethel, Jacob had a powerful vision where God promised him, "Your descendants will be like the dust of the earth, and you will spread out to the west and to the east, to the north and to the south. All peoples on earth will be blessed through you and your offspring" (Genesis 28:14).

Through Jacob's wives, Rachel and Leah, and their maids, God fulfills this promise. The two sisters are raised by a father, Laban, who treats them like barnyard animals which can be sold and bartered. They struggle with competition and comparison for much of their lives, but through God's compassion and love, both become women of faith.

How have you experienced Rachel and Leah as more than symbols and instead as real, living women through your study?

How might Rachel's and Leah's stories be different if they had found a way to complement each other rather than live in competition?

With whom do you have a Rachel-Leah relationship?

What creative steps can you take to celebrate rather than compete with that person?

What would it look like for you to practice abundant generosity, kindness, and forgiveness toward them?

What do you suspect would happen if you teamed up with this person rather than competed with this person?

TAMAR

*T*amar is an outsider, not part of the family made up of Abraham's descendants who will become the nation of Israel. Nevertheless, she is part of both David and Jesus' family tree. She's also an example of bold choices and of God's redemptive power in the midst of our messy lives.

—From *The Women of the Bible Speak*, **page 53**

Some stories in the Bible, like Tamar's, are a little tricky to teach in kids' Sunday school. With a checkered past and some strange, uncomfortable decisions and details, Tamar's story can seem easier to skip over. She's an outsider without any power or protector. She's forced to rely on ill-advised tactics to survive. Yet her story reveals that God specializes in making outsiders into insiders and redeeming our messes.

ℛEFLECT

The story of Tamar appears as a kind of interlude in Genesis 38. The previous chapter introduces the story of Joseph where he's betrayed by his brothers and sold to Potiphar. Immediately following Tamar's story, Genesis continues the story of Joseph, where he's betrayed by Potiphar's wife.

The Bible tells us the selling of Joseph was Judah's idea. Soon after, Judah leaves his brothers and settles among the Canaanites where he married Shua, and they have three sons.

Read Genesis 38:1–7. What does this passage reveal about Tamar's first husband, Er?

Though the Scripture does not specify, how do you think Er treated Tamar?

After Er's death, custom dictated that his wife marry his brother. This is known as a "leviratic" marriage—*levir* is Latin for "husband's brother"—and it was the custom among many Semitic peoples of the ancient Near East. Onan goes forward with the marriage, but he refuses to give Tamar a child. This may be because if Onan produces an heir for Er, it will decrease his inheritance.

Read Genesis 38:8–10. How does Onan treat Tamar?

What is God's response?

What does God's response reveal about how God sees and cares for Tamar?

Read Genesis 38:11. How does Judah see and respond to Tamar?

What do you think people whispered about Tamar after losing two husbands?

Tamar has no marriage, no future, no prospects of any kind of normal life. She's sent away as a dependent in her father's house until the day she dies. But she refuses to wallow in self-pity. Judah has done the wrong, and Tamar formulates a plan.

Read Genesis 38:12–23. How does Tamar trick Judah?

What does Tamar demand of Judah?

What is Judah most concerned with after the encounter? (Hint: v. 23)

Read Genesis 28:24–26. How does Judah respond to Tamar's pregnancy?

How does Judah change his response?

What does it suggest about Tamar's character that she chooses to send a message in private rather than publicly humiliate Judah?

Do you think you could have practiced such self-control? Why or why not?

Have you ever humiliated someone else in the process of pursuing justice? If so describe. What was the result?

Have you ever advocated for justice while avoiding a public humiliation of the offender? If so, describe. What was the result?

Read Genesis 38:27–30 and Matthew 1:2–3. What does it reveal about God that Tamar's little boy—son of an outsider, son of a Canaanite woman—becomes part of the royal line of the kingdom of Israel and Christ?

Remember: Tamar's story happens as an interlude in the middle of Joseph's story. Joseph is thrown into prison before rising to second-in-command of Egypt under Pharoah. When Jacob faces the possibility of sending his son, Benjamin, away, Judah steps forward and eventually offers his life to save his younger brother.

Read Genesis 43:8–9 and 44:33. How has Judah changed from the man who first suggested selling Joseph into slavery?

How do Tamar's actions force Judah to confront his own wrongdoing and show him how to be a person who stands for right when no one else has the courage?

What role does Tamar play in changing the angry, vengeful young man at the beginning of the story to the mature, compassionate man at the end?

CONNECT

Now that you've read and reflected on Tamar's story, it's time to connect this woman of the Bible with your life. Fill out the chart below.

What do you see as Tamar's greatest character strengths?	
What do you see as Tamar's greatest character weaknesses?	
Which strengths do you relate to or long for?	
Which weaknesses do you relate to or long to overcome?	
How do you hope to be more like Tamar in your faith journey?	

REVEAL

Now that you've connected with this woman of the Bible, it's time to look at how God reveals His presence to Tamar and how God is doing the same for you.

Where did you most see God show up in Tamar's life?	
What does God reveal about Himself and His character in the life of Tamar?	
Like Tamar, in what ways have you experienced God redeeming an impossible situation?	
How is God revealing Himself to you right now?	

$\mathscr{P}$RAY

Take a few minutes to ask the Holy Spirit to guide you as you respond to the following prayer prompts.

Lord, like Tamar, help me . . .

_____

_____

_____

Lord, whom am I tempted to publicly shame for their wrongdoing? How can I pursue justice without public humiliation?

_____

_____

_____

Lord, what's the injustice in which I most need Your wisdom in how to respond? How do You want me to respond?

_____

_____

_____

Lord, how can I be as wise as a serpent and innocent as a dove (Matthew 10:16)?

_____

_____

_____

Lord, considering Tamar's story, how are You calling me to live and respond to others differently?

_____

_____

_____

RUTH

*B*rave and momentous choices are everywhere in this story. Naomi's husband, Elimelech, left his homeland and made a new life for himself in Moab. Naomi chose to return home after his death. Ruth made the most daring choice of all, leaving her home and family to follow Naomi into the unknown.

—**From** *The Women of the Bible Speak*, **page 69**

For Ruth, life wasn't chock-full of the many choices we have today. For this woman to make such a radical choice—leaving her home country without any male protection and following Naomi to Judea—would have been almost unbelievable to early readers of this story. Yet Ruth's loyalty and determination transform her life and those around her. She teaches us a powerful lesson about the depths of God's love and the grace of His provision.

REFLECT

Like Tamar, Ruth is marked as an outsider from the beginning of her story. She marries a young Jewish man named Mahlon. Tragedy soon follows. Her father-in-law, Elimelech, dies, leaving her mother-in-law, Naomi, a widower. Then, her husband and his brother, Kilion, die, leaving Ruth and her sister-in-law Orpah, widowers, too. Ruth becomes part of a grieving trio: three women bound together by heartbreak, with extremely limited prospects for the future.

Read Ruth 1:1–5. What does this introduction to Ruth and her family reveal about them?

What losses do Ruth and her family members experience?

When have you experienced a series of heavy losses?

How did you respond?

Read Ruth 1:6–22. How does Naomi respond to this heartbreaking situation?

How does Ruth respond to her mother-in-law, Naomi?

What does this reveal about Ruth's character?

Scripture often shows us God favoring those willing to leave everything for His sake. What was the very first command God gave Abraham? "Go from your country, your people and your father's household," God said, "to the land I will show you" (Genesis 12:1). It's as if God sometimes has to pry us out of our comfort zones before He can accomplish His purposes through us. We often need to be jostled into a radical dependence on God before we can make real spiritual progress.

—From *The Women of the Bible Speak*, page 66

Read Ruth 2:1–12. In what specific ways does Boaz show kindness and generosity to Ruth?

How does Boaz's response to Ruth reflect God's response to His people? To you?

Toward whom are you showing outrageous kindness and generosity now?

Who is God nudging you to show kindness and generosity toward, but you've resisted?

What changes do you need to make in your attitudes and actions?

Boaz gives a foreigner, a woman, preferential treatment. Ruth is astonished at this generosity. In Ruth 2, we find another passage of compassionate words and actions when they are needed most.

Read Ruth 2:13–23. How does Boaz demonstrate hidden kindness to Ruth? (Hint: vv. 15–16)

Toward whom can you show hidden kindness this week?

Naomi soon hatches a plan: Ruth's marriage to Boaz. As a relative of Naomi's husband, he was in the position to act as a kinsman-redeemer, someone willing to marry a kinsman's widow and restore her position in the family. Marrying the wealthy Boaz would be a life-changing event for an impoverished immigrant like Ruth.

Read Ruth 3. What does Naomi instruct Ruth to do?

How does Boaz respond to Ruth?

What surprises you most about Boaz' response to Ruth?

Deeply impressed by Ruth, Boaz responds to the nobility of her nature. But before a marriage could take place, Boaz had to approach an unnamed male relative of Naomi who had first right of refusal to Naomi's property and her daughter-in-law, Ruth.

Read Ruth 4:1–12. How does Boaz redeem Ruth?

Read Ruth 4:13–15. How does Ruth's obedience and loyalty help save Naomi and her family?

Describe a time when you've seen God redeem a messy, impossible situation into something beautiful for yourself or others.

Early Christians, when they read the story of Ruth, couldn't help but see themselves in it. For them, it was more than just a nice story about a young woman who got her happy ending. Ruth's acceptance into the family of Israel spoke to them about their own inclusion in God's family. They found in this story an echo of Paul's words about the Gentile church, the "wild olive tree, were grafted in among them, and with them became a partaker of the root and fatness of the olive tree" (Romans 11:17 NKJV).

—From *The Women of the Bible Speak*, page 69

Where do you most need to experience God as your sustainer and the One who renews your life (Ruth 4:15)?

Read Ruth 4:18 and Matthew 1:5. What do these passages reveal about Ruth's child being in the lineage of Jesus?

How does Ruth experience blessing and reward for her loyalty toward Naomi and willingness to leave her land and gods?

CONNECT

Now that you've read and reflected on much of Ruth's story, it's time to connect this woman of the Bible with your life. Fill out the chart below.

What do you see as Ruth's greatest character strengths?	
What do you see as Ruth's greatest vulnerability?	
Which strengths do you relate to or long for?	
Which vulnerabilities do you relate to or long to overcome?	
How do you hope to be more like Ruth in your faith journey?	

REVEAL

Now that you've connected with this woman of the Bible, it's time to look at how God reveals His presence to Ruth and how God is doing the same for you.

Where did you most see God show up in Ruth's life?	
What does God reveal about Himself and His character through the losses and life of Ruth?	
Like Ruth, in what ways have you experienced the miraculous protection or provision of God?	
How is God showing His presence to you right now?	

PRAY

Take a few minutes to ask the Holy Spirit to guide you as you respond to the following prayer prompts.

Lord, like Ruth, help me . . .

_____

_____

Lord, toward whom are You calling me to show loyalty?

_____

_____

Lord, which family members or friends do You want me to rally around and support in their time of vulnerability or need?

_____

_____

Lord, how can I demonstrate Your lovingkindness toward them?

_____

_____

Lord, considering Ruth's story, how are You calling me to live differently?

_____

_____

*P*AIRS

We often look at women in the Bible on their own. By looking at them in pairs according to their relationships and life situations, we can better understand ourselves, God, and others.

Both Tamar and Ruth were outsiders, women grafted into the house of Israel. The Gospel of Matthew names Tamar and Ruth in the genealogy of Christ. God saw their value and worth as women and worked miracles through them.

How have you experienced Tamar and Ruth as more than symbols and instead as real, living women through your study?

How do Tamar's and Ruth's stories demonstrate the family of God is not built on blood, but on God's adoption of us, and our decision to choose God?

How do Tamar's and Ruth's stories demonstrate that in God's kingdom, the last will be first and the first will be last, and the despised and rejected will be the guests of greatest honor?

How does this give you with comfort and hope?

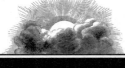

DEBORAH

One of the guiding stars God offers His people in the Book of Judges is His prophetess, Deborah. I have to tell you, she's one of my favorites. For me, the words of her story leap off the pages of my Bible. I find her brave and inspiring, and I'm pretty sure I would have followed her into battle. This was a woman with guts and wisdom, a role model for the ages.

—**From** *The Women of the Bible Speak*, **page 78**

*D*eborah, whose name means "bee," delivers quite a sting! She's selected and equipped by God to lead during a crucial time in the history of the Israelites. Though the army faces impossible odds, she rises as a prophetess and military leader. Her discernment, bravery, and willingness to deliver hard news helps rescue God's people both spiritually and physically.

ℛEFLECT

The book of Judges challenges us, because it shows the reality of God's children wandering away. The Israelites have received so much by God. They've been fed and led through the desert. They've watched the wall of Jericho crumble. Yet they stray from God. Each time they're lured away, God draws them back, often using the oppression of their enemies to do it.

When we catch up with the Israelites in Judges 4, they're ruled by Jabin, the rich, powerful king of Canaan. The Israelites cry out to God, and that's when we meet Deborah.

Read Judges 4:4–5. How is Deborah introduced in the Bible?

What does this introduction hint about her leadership style?

Read Judges 4:6–7. What are Deborah's instructions to the warrior, Barak?

Which of the following characteristics does Deborah demonstrate as a leader? Circle all that apply.

Hesitance   Confidence   Fearfulness   Poise

Strength   Foolishness   Faithfulness   Courage

Read Judges 4:8–10. How does Barak's response compare with Deborah's response?

Where are you resisting God's call or leading because you feel ill-equipped?

Read Judges 4:11–16. What's miraculous about this victory?

As a prophetess and judge, Deborah oversees a powerful victory. In response, she and Barak create one of the longest poetic compositions in the Bible. Their song echoes that of Moses and Israelites after crossing through the Red Sea.

Read Judges 5:1–11. What characteristics of God are celebrated and credited in this song?

When you experience a win or success, what do you attribute it to other than God?

How can you be more like Deborah and Barak and reflect on the character of God in your gratitude?

Deborah changes the course of history and brings something to the land that they'd lost.

Read Judges 5:31. What is the result of Deborah's obedience?

How does this contrast with where the story began? (Hint: Judges 5:3)

Describe a time when you knew God was fighting on your behalf.

How did this strengthen your faith? Your leadership? Your character?

Where is God calling you to rise up in bravery and obedience?

What's holding you back from responding to that call?

CONNECT

Now that you've read and reflected on much of Deborah's story, it's time to connect this woman of the Bible with your life. Fill out the chart below.

What do you see as Deborah's greatest character strengths?	
What do you see as Deborah's greatest gift as a leader?	
Which strengths do you relate to or long for?	
Which leadership gifts can you relate to or long to experience?	
How do you hope to be more like Deborah in your faith journey?	

Reveal

Now that you've connected with this woman of the Bible, it's time to look at how God reveals His nature to Deborah and how God is doing the same for you.

Where did you most see God show up in Deborah's life?	
What does God reveal about Himself and His character in the life of Deborah?	
Like Deborah, in what ways have you experienced God calling you to speak up and lead well?	
How is God revealing Himself to you right now?	

$\mathscr{P}$RAY

Take a few minutes to ask the Holy Spirit to guide you as you respond to the following prayer prompts.

Lord, like Deborah, help me . . .

_____

_____

Lord, where are You calling me to speak up in confidence and truth?

_____

_____

Lord, where are You calling me to step out in faith and trust You for the victory?

_____

_____

_____

Lord, how do You want to use me to bring peace?

_____

_____

_____

Lord, considering Deborah's story, how are You calling me to live differently?

_____

_____

_____

JAEL

Just as God had prepared and established Deborah to right His people and lead them to victory, Jael was positioned exactly where God needed her to be to give His people the upper hand and a final victory over Jabin. In the battles He sets before us, God expects us to fight as Jael did, with the weapons we have.

—**From** *The Women of the Bible Speak*, **page 96**

*L*ike Tamar and Ruth, Jael is considered an outsider. Yet she bravely kills a man who has cruelly oppressed the Israelites for two decades. Her actions cap off an unexpected, momentous victory by Israel that launches its people into a new era of peace.

*R*EFLECT

Deborah, about whom we just read, sets the stage for Jael. When Deborah prophesizes to Barak about the battle Israel is about to win, Barak balks and says that if Deborah doesn't join him on the battlefield, then he's not going.

"Certainly I will go with you," said Deborah. "But because of the course you are taking, the honor will not be yours, for the LORD **will deliver Sisera into the hands of a woman**" (Judges 4:9).

Barak didn't trust the word of the Lord, and so God uses an unsuspecting woman, Jael, to defeat the mighty commander, Sisera. After his army is destroyed, Sisera retreats and finds himself in the tent of Jael.

Read Judges 4:17–20. How does Jael make Sisera feel safe and provided for?

What does Sisera ask of Jael?

How would you respond if a military commander wanted to hide in your house and make you stand at the door?

Read Judges 4:21. What does Jael do to Sisera when he's sleeping?

How does Jael's action become a turning point in the battle?

Read Judges 4:22–24. What do you think Barak thought and felt when he realized Deborah's prophesy had been fulfilled (vv. 7–9)?

How do Barak and Jael compare and contrast as leaders?

> We know nothing of what Jael's life was like before this, but it seems she must have felt some level of sympathy for the people of Israel. Had she seen the brutal treatment they'd suffered at the hands of Jabin and Sisera? Was she simply moved by the Spirit of God to rescue His people after they cried out to Him? After all, He had provided for Deborah, and they bravely followed her leadership into battle.
>
> —From *The Women of the Bible Speak*, page 85

Reflecting on this story, do you think Jael already formulated a plan in her head before Sisera even said a word or acted on impulse? Explain.

Jael risked everything to throw her lot in with the people of Israel. When have you risked everything to throw your lot in with God and His people?

What was the result?

Read Judges 5:24–27. How is Jael described in Deborah and Barak's song?

Where is God calling you to fight against oppression or injustice with the weapons you have?

CONNECT

Now that you've read and reflected on much of Jael's story, it's time to connect this woman of the Bible with your own life. Fill out the chart below.

What do you see as Jael's greatest character strengths?	
What do you see as Jael's greatest character weaknesses?	
Which strengths do you relate to or long for?	
Which weaknesses do you relate to or long to overcome?	
How do you hope to be more like Jael in your faith journey?	

REVEAL

Now that you've connected with this woman of the Bible, it's time to look at how God reveals His character and strength to Jael and how God is doing the same for you.

Where did you most see God show up in Jael's life?	
What does God reveal about Himself and His character in the life of Jael?	
Like Jael, in what ways have you experienced God positioning you to be used in the right time and right way for His glory?	
How is God revealing Himself to you right now?	

$\mathscr{P}$RAY

Take a few minutes to ask the Holy Spirit to guide you as you respond to the following prayer prompts.

Lord, like Jael, help me . . .

_____

_____

_____

Lord, against which areas of injustice are You calling me to fight? What's the weapon You're calling me to use?

_____

_____

_____

Lord, where am I most tempted by timidity and hesitation? How can I walk in greater courage?

_____

_____

_____

Lord, how can I join in the work You're already doing in the world?

_____

_____

_____

Lord, considering Jael's story, how are You calling me to live differently?

_____

_____

_____

$\mathcal{P}$AIRS

We often look at women in the Bible on their own. By looking at them in pairs, according to their relationships and life situations, we can better understand ourselves, God, and others.

Both Deborah and Jael take decisive action when God places them in positions to lead and to act. Unlike Barak, who has qualms about leading the army of Israel, neither of these women are hesitant or reluctant. Just as God prepares and establishes Deborah to save His people and lead them to victory, God prepares and positions Jael to give His people the upper hand and final victory.

Who are you more like: the prophetess Deborah or the warrior Jael? Explain.

On a scale of one to ten, how ready and armed do you feel for an assignment from God?

How do the stories of Deborah and Jael turn expectations regarding women and leadership on their heads?

Read Ephesians 6:10–18. What is the armor that God calls you to wear and what weapons does He call you to carry?

How does each of the pieces of armor help position and prepare you to be used powerfully by God like Deborah and Jael?

HANNAH

In order to have David, we have to have Samuel, the prophet who anointed David to his great calling. And to have Samuel, we have to have Hannah. So, Hannah stands right at the center of this unfolding story. Once again, a woman is included in the pages of the Bible not only as a central character in the dramatic adventure that leads us to the arrival of our Savior, but also to teach us important lessons about faithfulness and redemption in the midst of pain.

—**From** *The Women of the Bible Speak*, **page 103**

*I*n the ancient world, childbirth gave women value and was viewed as a sign of God's favor. Like Sarah and Rachel, Hannah struggles with infertility. She's harassed for her barrenness. Yet rather than let the mockery get to her, she teaches us that our pain can drive us to the only source who can help us—God.

REFLECT

Elkanah has two wives, Peninnah and Hannah. Peninnah has children, but Hannah has none. Every year, Elkanah, travels to Shiloh to worship and offer a sacrifice to God.

Read 1 Samuel 1:1–5. How does Elkanah show his affection and compassion toward Hannah through his offering?

What's the biggest unfulfilled desire of your heart?

Who are three people God used to show you kindness or compassion in your unfulfilled longing?

Who are three people with an unfulfilled longing to whom you can show kindness and compassion?

❖ _____

❖ _____

❖ _____

What's worse than an unmet longing is someone who leverages that ache by taunting and one-upping us in that area of pain. That's what Hannah faced with Elkanah's other wife. Peninnah wasn't satisfied to find contentment in her own full life; she had to rub Hannah's face in it, hit her where her heart ached most.

Read 1 Samuel 1:6–7. Which best describes how Hannah felt about the other wife's treatment of her? Circle all that apply.

Encouraged	Isolated	Crushed	Happy
Alone	Discouraged	Appreciated	Dismissed
Mocked	Hopeful	Attacked	Anguished

Name the biggest rival or nemesis in your life.

How has that person treated you or caused pain?

What loss or pain might be in that person's life or past that causes them to hurt others?

Read 1 Samuel 1:8. How does Elkanah express tender care and concern for Hannah?

Read 1 Samuel 1:9–11. How does Hannah respond (or not respond) to her rival?

To whom does she take her pain and longing?

How are you responding (or not responding) to your rival or nemesis?

To whom are you taking your pain and longing?

What can you learn from Hannah's response?

What pledge does Hannah prayerfully make to God?

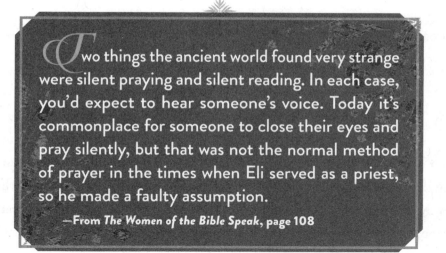

Two things the ancient world found very strange were silent praying and silent reading. In each case, you'd expect to hear someone's voice. Today it's commonplace for someone to close their eyes and pray silently, but that was not the normal method of prayer in the times when Eli served as a priest, so he made a faulty assumption.

—From *The Women of the Bible Speak*, page 108

Read 1 Samuel 1:12–14. How does Eli add salt to Hannah's wounds by falsely accusing her?

When has someone misread or misunderstood you in your weakest, most desperate moment?

When have you misread or misunderstood someone else in their weakest, most desperate moment?

How did you make the relationship right again?

Read 1 Samuel 1:15–20. What blessing does Hannah receive and how does God answer her prayers and petitions?

Hannah names her firstborn Samuel—"Shemu-el," in Hebrew for "God had heard." During the time she nurses and raises him, she holds back from going with the rest of the family on the yearly pilgrimage to Shiloh. But once Samuel reaches the age of weaning, she packs up her most precious treasure and brings her baby boy back to Shiloh, the very place she so fervently prayed for a child.

Read 1 Samuel 1:24–28. How does Hannah fulfill her prayerful pledge to God?

What precious gift are you clinging to too tightly that you need to give over to God?

Read 1 Samuel 2:1–2. What does this passage reveal about Hannah's attitude toward giving her most precious son to God?

Read 1 Samuel 2:3–10. What characteristics of God does Hannah highlight throughout her song of praise?

When it comes to your unfulfilled desires, which of these characteristics of God have been most meaningful? Why?

> Hannah's God is the God of reversal. He upended death. He alone could humble and exalt. He took people who had nothing and gave them everything. She had lived this reality, and her view of God's infinite power was broader than her own little hill village of Ramathaim. Hannah also put a spotlight on a truth we see again and again in Scripture: that God's ways are not the ways of the world.
>
> —From *The Women of the Bible Speak*, page 112

Read 1 Samuel 2:18–21. How does Hannah continue to show her love for Samuel? (Hint: v. 19)

How does God continue to honor and bless Hannah and Elkanah?

Through Hannah's faithfulness and God's blessing, she gets to watch Samuel grow into a great prophet, one who served God and would one day anoint King David to lead His people.

CONNECT

Now that you've read and reflected on much of Hannah's story and various mentions of her throughout the Bible, it's time to connect this woman of the Bible with your own life. Fill out the chart below.

What do you see as Hannah's greatest character strengths?	
What do you see as Hannah's greatest character weaknesses?	
Which strengths do you relate to or long for?	
Which weaknesses do you relate to or long to overcome?	
How do you hope to be more like Hannah in your faith journey?	

REVEAL

Now that you've connected with this woman of the Bible, it's time to look at how God reveals His presence to Hannah and how God is doing the same for you.

Where did you most see God show up in Hannah's life?	
What does God reveal about Himself and His character in the life of Hannah?	
Like Hannah, in what ways have you experienced the faithfulness of God?	
How is God revealing Himself to you right now?	

$\mathscr{P}$RAY

Take a few minutes to ask the Holy Spirit to guide you as you respond to the following prayer prompts.

Lord, like Hannah, help me . . .

_____

_____

_____

Lord, who has been unkind toward me in my pain? Toward whom have I been unkind in their pain? What are You calling me to do to heal and restore these relationships?

_____

_____

_____

Lord, what's the wound or need deep in my life that, like Hannah, I need to lay at Your feet?

_____

_____

_____

Lord, what's the relationship that seems beyond repair, the financial hole, the unfulfilled longing, the dream that seems will never become a reality that's holding me back from You? How can I trust You with this?

_____

_____

_____

Lord, considering Hannah's story, how are You calling me to live differently?

_____

_____

_____

MIRIAM

The Bible doesn't tell us clearly whether Miriam married or had children of her own. Her life was, though, dedicated to her people and their survival, starting with her brother Moses, the very man who would lead his people out of Egypt and away from the crushing bonds of centuries of slavery. This daring woman was called "Miriam the prophetess" (Exodus 15:20). Very few women in the Bible have the title, because to be a prophet meant not just to speak the word of the Lord, but also to lead the people into hearing and accepting that truth.

—**From** *The Women of the Bible Speak*, **page 116**

On the riverbank of the Nile, Miriam boldly steps into a life-threatening situation regarding her brother, Moses, and helps save him. Later, after Moses leads God's people across the Red Sea, Miriam the prophetess, grabs the tambourine and leads the people into exuberant worship for God's faithfulness. Miriam isn't a perfect leader, but she shows us that even when we make mistakes, nothing is beyond God's redemption.

REFLECT

From a young age, Miriam kept an eye on her younger brother, Moses, and plays a crucial role in protecting him.

Read Exodus 2:1–10. What role does Miriam play in saving her brother, Moses?

How do you think Jochebed felt when Miriam ran to tell her the news?

What godly characteristics does Miriam display through this passage?

Name two people you have watched over or helped save from sticky situations for over the years.

✿ _____

✿ _____

List one way that each of those relationships has shaped you.

✿ _____

✿ _____

Moses may have carried some memories of his Hebrew family with him into Pharaoh's palace. Because of his time with his birth family, he knew who he was, and he came to identify with his people. It's what prompts Moses, years later, to intervene when he sees an Egyptian beating a Hebrew slave. After Moses kills the abuser, he retreats to the desert where God calls him to speak out against Pharoah.

Through a series of miracles, God's people are set free, and Moses is reunited with his family. After the miraculous crossing of the Red Sea, Miriam appears as a leader of the people and reaches for a musical instrument and turns their joy into exuberant dance.

Read Exodus 15:20–21. How is the now-grown-up, big sister of Moses, Miriam, introduced in this passage?

What actions and characteristics of God does Miriam celebrate through worship?

Where has God been most reliable in your biggest struggles?

Where has God shown up, even if it wasn't in the way you anticipated or planned?

Write a chorus of worship and thanksgiving in the space below.

Later Miriam the prophetess, Aaron the priest, Moses the leader, and the rest of the Israelites find themselves wandering through the desert. Their hope slowly erodes. Miriam and Aaron express their dissent.

Read Numbers 12:1–9. What complaint do Miriam and her brother make about Moses?

How does God respond?

Which of the following do you think compels Miriam and Aaron to complain about Moses? Place a check (√) by each one.

_____ Judgmentalism   _____ Ambition   _____ Jealousy

_____ Anger   _____ Envy   _____ Other

Which of these are you struggling with most today?

What are you being tempted to do in response that may be rash or harmful?

Read Numbers 12:10. What happens to Miriam?

What does this reveal about Miriam being the ringleader of the dissent?

Read Numbers 12:11–16. How do Miriam's brothers respond when they see her suffering?

Aaron:

Moses:

What does this reveal about Miriam's importance to her brothers and to the Israelites?

How do Moses and Aaron intercede in prayer for their sister?

Name up to three people who intercede in prayer for you.

* _____

* _____

* _____

Name three people for whom you interceded (or want to intercede) in prayer.

* _____

* _____

* _____

Who is someone new for whom God is nudging you to start interceding in prayer?

> At no point in the quarrel, punishment, and reconciliation did God treat Miriam as anything other than a prophetess who had made a mistake, despite the fact that her sin played out so publicly. Her leadership of the people was not questioned. Miriam was still Miriam, respected by both God and her people.
>
> —From *The Women of the Bible Speak*, page 124–125

What does Miriam's story reveal about being wrong and yet redeemed?

What hope does this give you about your past or present mistakes?

Reflecting on Miriam's story, do your past mistakes tend to refine you or define you?

How can you allow God to use these experiences to refine you?

Scripture tells us little more about Miriam except a brief note of her death (Numbers 20:1), yet she played a crucial role in rescuing Moses and the Israelites.

CONNECT

Now that you've read and reflected on much of Miriam's story, it's time to connect this woman of the Bible with your own life. Fill out the chart below.

What do you see as Miriam's greatest character strengths?	
What do you see as Miriam's greatest character weaknesses?	
Which strengths do you relate to or long for?	
Which weaknesses do you relate to or long to overcome?	
How do you hope to be more like Miriam in your faith journey?	

REVEAL

Now that you've connected with this woman of the Bible, it's time to look at how God showed His presence to Miriam and how God is doing the same for you.

Where did you most see God show up in Miriam's life?	
What does God reveal about Himself and His character in the life of Miriam?	
Like Miriam, in what ways have you experienced God using you in significant ways?	
How is God revealing Himself to you right now?	

𝒫RAY

Take a few minutes to ask the Holy Spirit to guide you as you respond to the following prayer prompts.

Lord, like Miriam, help me . . .

_____

_____

Lord, on whom are You calling me to rescue, protect, or keep an eye?

_____

_____

Lord, what's one area of my life over which I most need to break out in joyful worship?

_____

_____

Lord, where am I most tempted by ambition or jealousy to take control of a situation? How can I trust You more?

_____

_____

Lord, considering Miriam's story, how are You calling me to live differently?

_____

_____

$\mathscr{P}$AIRS

We often look at women in the Bible on their own. By looking at them in pairs, according to their relationships and life situations, we can better understand ourselves, God, and others.

Hannah and Miriam each watch as a treasured, beloved family member is given to the Lord for His greater plans and purposes. Hannah watches her beloved son, Samuel, walk off into the care of Eli, knowing she might see him once a year, at best.

Miriam, too, watches as Moses launches into unknown territory, first into the Nile and then into the palace of Pharaoh, never knowing when or if she might reunite with her precious brother. Both women had close relationships with God, trusting, praying, and relying on His promises. Both had front-row seats to incredible miracles. God reaches down into each of their lives and does what was impossible with human effort.

How have you experienced Hannah and Miriam as more than symbols and instead as real, living women through your study?

Do you relate more to Hannah or Miriam? Why?

When have you experienced the deep rejoicing, like Hannah and Miriam, that comes from living in close relationship with God?

What role does praise and worship play in changing your attitude or perspective toward God and others?

Esther

This is exactly where a good novel should end: The beautiful young heroine has achieved the pinnacle of earthly glory and has triumphed. But that is not the end of Esther's story—instead, it's just the beginning. Because this is a story about heavenly glory, not earthly glory. It's a story about God's love for His people and about the courage this young woman found the moment it was most needed.

—**From** *The Women of the Bible Speak*, **pages 135–136**

Other than Ruth, Esther is the only other woman with a book of the Bible named after her. Esther's story is unusual. It's the longest of any woman in Scripture and it takes place entirely outside of Israel. Yet through Esther we discover God's perfect timing and orchestrating presence behind the scenes.

ℛEFLECT

The story of Esther has all the makings of a Hollywood blockbuster. The emperor of Persia, King Xerxes, hosts a great feast and summons his wife, Queen Vashti, wishing to display her beauty to the nobles. She refuses to come, and the angry king divorces her on the spot. The king soon holds an unusual beauty contest to select a new queen. Esther is drafted into the pageant. Her older cousin, Mordecai, who took her in as an orphan after her parents' death, instructs her not to reveal her nationality or family.

Read Esther 2:8–16. If you were Esther, what aspects of this regimen and treatment would you enjoy?

If you were Esther, with what aspects of this regimen and treatment would you struggle?

Read Esther 2:17–20. Knowing that Esther, with the support of Mordecai, will one day save God's people, how do the events in this passage set the stage for their position and favor?

Reflecting on your life, when has God used a moment of favor or success to position you to bring Him glory?

Read Esther 3:2–6. What does Mordecai refuse to do and how does Haman respond?

How are you being tempted to bow to something or someone other than God?

Do you have anyone, like Haman, who is angered by your faith?

How are you navigating the situation?

> *B*owing in the Persian context didn't mean a slight tip of the head or a gentle curtsey. It meant full prostration. It was a gesture also familiar to ancient Jews, but with one difference: That kind of bow was reserved for God alone. Only in the Temple and only to God would a Jew make such a gesture of ultimate submission. Haman hated Mordecai because the Jewish man wouldn't show him that kind of deference. So, the plot that Haman hatched, to exterminate every Jew in the empire, had at its root Haman's hatred for Jews and the God they worshipped.
>
> —From *The Women of the Bible Speak*, pages 136–137

Read Esther 3:8–13. What cruelty and racism does Haman show through his plan?

When have you been on the receiving end of someone's cruelty or racism?

When have you been cruel or racist toward someone else?

How can you go back and make the situation right?

When Mordecai hears about the proposed genocide for his people, he begins grieving, and doing so very publicly. Esther sends clothes to the one who has raised her like a father, but he refuses them. She sends one of her royal attendants to find out why he's so troubled, and Mordecai sends back a message with chilling details.

Read Esther 4:7–17. What surprises you about Esther's response to Mordecai?

How does she lay a foundation of faith among God's people?

Describe a time you experienced the effectiveness of collective prayer.

What role does prayer and fasting play in your spiritual life?

How would you have responded if you were in Esther's situation?

In what ways are you in Esther's situation now?

What's one way God is nudging you to speak up and act on behalf of others today?

How are you responding?

Esther eventually hosts a banquet in which she makes her plea known to the king and Haman overhears.

Read Esther 7. How does the king respond to Esther's request?

How does the king respond to Haman?

Where do you long to see God's justice?

Read Esther 8:11–17. How does the king's decree protect and provide for the Jewish people?

What do the Jewish people experience? (Hint: v. 16–17)

How do those who witness this miracle respond? (Hint: v. 17)

How did God use Esther's courage and resourcefulness to bring salvation?

Though God's name is never mentioned in the book of Esther, how is God working behind the scenes?

How do you suspect God is working behind the scenes in your life?

CONNECT

Now that you've read and reflected on much of Esther's story, it's time to connect this woman of the Bible with your life. Fill out the chart below.

What do you see as Esther's greatest character strengths?	
What do you see as Esther's greatest temptations or struggles?	
Which strengths do you relate to or long for?	
Which temptations or struggles do you relate to or long to overcome?	
How do you hope to be more like Esther in your faith journey?	

REVEAL

Now that you've connected with this woman of the Bible, it's time to look at how God is working behind the scenes through Esther and how God is doing the same for you.

Where did you most see God show up in Esther's life?	
What does God reveal about Himself and His character through the life of Esther?	
Like Esther, in what ways have you seen God's handiwork in your life?	
How is God revealing Himself to you right now?	

$\mathcal{P}$RAY

Take a few minutes to ask the Holy Spirit to guide you as you respond to the following prayer prompts.

Lord, like Esther, help me . . .

_____

_____

_____

Lord, how have You been positioning me to love, bless, and protect others?

_____

_____

_____

Lord, where's my current "for such a time as this" moment? What do I need to do quickly in obedience to You?

_____

_____

_____

Lord, where do I most need to rally faithful friends to pray?

_____

_____

_____

Lord, considering Esther's story, how are You calling me to live differently?

_____

_____

_____

RAHAB

Rahab's name points us to some important truths about her. In Hebrew, her name is *Rachav*, meaning "He enlarges" or "He widens." It was a common image of fruitfulness: God enlarging the womb of a pregnant woman, thickening the ear of grain, making the fruit to swell and burst. In Rahab's case, the name has another meaning: to enlarge a land area. Because of her bravery at a critical moment, that's exactly what she helped Israel to do—and that was just the beginning! Rahab the prostitute is one of the ancestors of Christ Himself.

—**From** *The Women of the Bible Speak*, **page 144**

A peasant and pagan from an ancient Canaanite town, Rahab manages to survive working as an innkeeper and prostitute. Yet she's the reason Joshua's army makes its very first conquest, the city of Jericho, and therefore plays an essential role in Israel's later glory and prosperity. Rahab teaches us that great bravery can come at the most unexpected times and ways.

ℛEFLECT

After forty years of wandering in the desert, Moses dies. Joshua must now lead the Israelites into the Promised Land. But it wouldn't come without a struggle. The land of Canaan had trained warriors and fortified cities. To better understand what they're up against, Joshua sends out a group of spies who end up on at Rahab's front door.

Read Joshua 2:1–3. In what tough position does Rahab find herself?

Read Joshua 2:4–7. What surprises you most about the way Rahab responds to the king of Jericho's orders?

How would you have responded if placed in the same situation?

What have you recently done to protect someone else?

What was the result?

Read Joshua 2:8–11. What actions and characteristics of God had Rahab heard about before the spies arrived?

How did this change her political and spiritual allegiances?

Why did Rahab make what appeared to be an impulsive choice, to lie to the soldiers of her own king, putting herself and her entire family at tremendous risk?

How would you describe Rahab's faith?

How is Rahab's fear of God different from the fear of Jericho's king?

Read Joshua 2:12–14. How does Rahab shrewdly negotiate with the spies?

What is their response?

Read Joshua 2:15–24. How do the spies shrewdly negotiate with Rahab?

Like Rahab, we all have to experience a moment when we fully understand the reality of God and His power to redeem us. It's the gift of faith, a gift Rahab was clearly given. Her profession, her nationality—nothing on the surface would have appeared to put her on the path to becoming a part of the nation of Israel and into the lineage of Jesus Himself. Yet God expertly crafted her story, leading Israel's brave spies to her doorstep and giving her courage when she needed it most.

—From *The Women of the Bible Speak*, page 148

Read Joshua 6:20–25. How are Rahab and her family spared?

What do Rahab and your experience of salvation have in common?

From what have you been saved?

Like the scarlet cord, what marks you as God's possession?

Read Matthew 1:5, Hebrews 11:31, and James 2:25–26. How is Rahab celebrated and remembered in the New Testament?

CONNECT

Now that you've read and reflected on much of Rahab's story and various mentions of her throughout the Bible, it's time to connect this woman of the Bible with your own life. Fill out the chart below.

What do you see as Rahab's greatest character strengths?	
What do you see as Rahab's greatest character weaknesses?	
Which strengths do you relate to or long for?	
Which weaknesses do you relate to or long to overcome?	
How do you hope to be more like Rahab in your faith journey?	

ℛEVEAL

Now that you've connected with this woman of the Bible, it's time to look at how God works through Rahab and how God is doing the same with you.

Where did you most see God show up in Rahab's life?	
What does God reveal about Himself and His character in the life of Rahab?	
Like Rahab, in what ways has God called you to respond to His faithfulness with great courage?	
How is God revealing Himself to you right now?	

$\mathscr{P}$RAY

Take a few minutes to ask the Holy Spirit to guide you as you respond to the following prayer prompts.

Lord, like Rahab, help me . . .

_____

_____

_____

Lord, whom are You calling me to defend or protect? How can I protect the defenseless for Your glory?

_____

_____

_____

Lord, where am I most tempted to give into fear rather than step into greater faith?

_____

_____

_____

Lord, for what are You asking me to lay down my life?

_____

_____

_____

Lord, considering Rahab's story, how are You calling me to live differently?

_____

_____

_____

$\mathcal{P}$AIRS

We often look at women in the Bible on their own. By looking at them in pairs, according to their relationships and life situations, we can better understand ourselves, God, and others.

Esther and Rahab make an unlikely pair: one a queen, the other a prostitute. They lived seven hundred years apart—Esther during the exile in Babylon and Persia, and Rahab at Israel's founding as a nation. Yet both women are critical to the survival of God's people, placed divinely into position, and called upon to step up in a moment of courage.

How have you experienced Esther and Rahab as more than symbols and instead as real, living women through your study?

How might Esther's and Rahab's stories be different if they had responded in fear rather than risk everything at the opportune time?

Both Esther and Rahab make bold decisions. What's one bold decision you sense God asking you to make?

What's holding you back?

MARY OF BETHANY

Mary's unreserved expression of love toward Jesus may not have been logical by the standards of her time, but it serves as a clear example of her unabashedly following Him in a way that others deemed foolish. She was willing to break with tradition to do what was most important: learn from and honor her Savior. Sitting at the master's feet in a group of men? Ignoring a woman's expected duties? Making a spectacle of herself by anointing Jesus' feet and wiping them with her hair, of all things? Mary lived out a key lesson: It's not the world's approval we should be chasing.

—**From** *The Women of the Bible Speak*, **page 160**

*I*n many of Mary of Bethany's interactions, she focuses on Jesus. Whether sitting at the feet of Christ drinking in His rich teachings or scandalously letting down her hair to anoint His body for burial, she gives us a stunning portrait of what devotion to Jesus can look like.

REFLECT

Mary of Bethany reminds us to never allow the busyness of service to distract us from the goal of loving God with all our hearts, souls, and minds. This requires spending time with Him listening, praying, meditating on His words—not just running through a list of to-do's.

Read Luke 10:38–42. How does Mary posture herself physically and spiritually before Jesus?

What does this reveal about her spiritual hunger and attitude toward Jesus?

What does it look like for you to love Jesus with your whole mind, heart, body, and strength?

How do you show attentiveness and affection for Jesus in your daily life?

How does Martha criticize Mary?

How does Jesus defend Mary?

Mary of Bethany also makes a striking appearance just before Jesus' entrance into Jerusalem. Everything that happened that week played out on a very public stage: the crowds crying, "Hosanna," the teaching in the Temple, the driving out of the money changers, the arrest in the garden. It was a whirlwind of a week, and ended in the most public expression of violence known in the Roman world: crucifixion. What followed is Jesus' triumph over sin and death, His sealing of salvation for all who will accept it. But before all that, Jesus shares an intimate time with His close friends in Bethany.

—From *The Women of the Bible Speak*, page 157

Read John 12:1–3. How does Mary express affection and intimate worship of Jesus?

What does affection and intimate worship of Jesus look like for you?

What holds you back from expressing your affection and worship of Jesus more fully or frequently?

How concerned is Mary of Bethany with what others think about her vulnerable adoration?

When you worship Jesus, are you more concerned about what others think or what Jesus thinks?

Read John 12:4–8. How does Judas criticize Mary of Bethany?

How does Jesus defend Mary of Bethany?

What does Jesus' defense of Mary with Martha and Jesus' defense of Mary with Judas have in common?

When someone criticizes your faith or response to Jesus, do you allow Jesus to defend you or take matters into your own hands and try to defend yourself?

What motivates your response?

What does Mary challenge you to do more of and less of through her example?

CONNECT

Now that you've read and reflected on much of Mary of Bethany's story, it's time to connect this woman of the Bible with your life. Fill out the chart below.

What do you see as Mary's greatest character strengths?	
What do you see as Mary's greatest character weaknesses?	
Which strengths do you relate to or long for?	
Which weaknesses do you relate to or long to overcome?	
How do you hope to be more like Mary in your faith journey?	

REVEAL

Now that you've connected with this woman of the Bible, it's time to look at how Jesus reveals His love to Mary of Bethany and how Jesus is doing the same for you.

Where did you most see Jesus show up in Mary's life?	
What does Jesus reveal about Himself and His character in the life of Mary?	
Like Mary, in what ways have you experienced and expressed unabashed affection and worship of Jesus?	
How is Jesus revealing Himself to you right now?	

𝒫RAY

Take a few minutes to ask the Holy Spirit to guide you as you respond to the following prayer prompts.

Lord, like Mary of Bethany, help me . . .

_____

_____

_____

Lord, how am I currently distracted from adoring and worshipping You? How can I take more time to simply be with You?

_____

_____

_____

Lord, where am I most tempted to try to defend myself? How can I trust You more as my defender?

_____

_____

_____

Lord, where are You asking me to trust you more?

_____

_____

_____

Lord, considering Mary of Bethany's story, how are You calling me to live differently?

MARTHA

*I*n her faith and trust, Martha believed it would never be too late for God to act. Her confidence in Jesus was boundless, and she alone seemed to realize—perhaps she alone in all of John's Gospel—that Jesus was not bound by considerations of space and time, but participated fully in the timeless life of God.

—**From** *The Women of the Bible Speak*, **page 167**

All too often, Martha is judged by a single interaction with Jesus during a hectic dinner party. She's dismissed as a busy bee, more concerned with doing *for* Jesus than being *with* Jesus. But this is a shallow, dismissive assessment of a powerhouse of a woman and misses her remarkable faith and faithfulness.

REFLECT

In the famous story of Mary and Martha hosting Jesus, we often miss all the good things that Martha did for Jesus and how much she loved Him, too.

Read Luke 10:38–42. What does it communicate about Martha's character and love of Jesus that she's the one who opens their house to Jesus?

What does it communicate about Martha's character and love of Jesus that she's preparing so much for His visit?

What does it suggest about Martha's relationship with Jesus that she brought her area of disappointment and pain directly to Him?

When you're frustrated by someone's action or lack of action, do you tend to take your concern to the person, to Jesus, or to someone else? Explain.

Have you ever worn yourself out by doing for God without taking time to be with God? What was the result?

How do you find a healthy balance between cultivating your relationship with Jesus and serving Him?

Jesus responded to her with infinite tenderness. He didn't answer in anger, but with care for her soul and an ear for her frustration. He identified her state—worried and troubled—and gently showed her a better path. Take notice of the unique way He begins His response: "Martha, Martha," He says to her, and with those words, she becomes one of only three people in the New Testament whom Jesus addresses in the emphatic, doubled form of her name.

—From *The Women of the Bible Speak*, page 165

What does it communicate about Jesus' love of Martha that He would call her to deeper discipleship in a way that may not come naturally to her?

What are three ways Jesus is calling you to deeper discipleship in ways that may not come easily to you?

✿ _____

✿ _____

✿ _____

Later, when Martha and Mary's brother, Lazarus, dies, the sisters interact with Jesus in two very different ways that highlight their strengthens and weaknesses.

Read John 11:1–5. How does Jesus feel about Martha and her sister according to verse 5?

What do you think John is highlighting about Martha when He lists Martha first and does not name her sister in verse 5?

Read John 11:17–21. How does Martha demonstrate her love of Jesus?

How does Martha's response to Jesus demonstrate the depths of her faith and trust in Jesus?

Read John 11:22–27. How does Jesus reveal His identity to Martha?

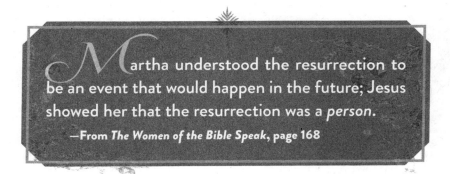

*M*artha understood the resurrection to be an event that would happen in the future; Jesus showed her that the resurrection was a *person.*

—From *The Women of the Bible Speak*, page 168

What does Martha's response to Jesus' "I Am" statement have in common with Peter's response to Jesus in Matthew 16:16?

What's one situation you're tempted to believe it's too late for God to act?

Read John 11:28–32. How does Martha show love and concern for her sister?

How do the sisters' responses differ? Fill in your responses below.

❀ Martha's response and expression of faith:

❀ Mary's response and expression of faith:

Read John 11:38–44. What practical concern does Martha express?

How does Jesus lead Martha back to her own statement of faith? (Hint: v. 40)

How does Jesus reveal Himself as the resurrection and the life?

What's one impossible situation in your life that only Jesus can make possible?

Where do you most need to experience Jesus as the resurrection and the life?

CONNECT

Now that you've read and reflected on much of Martha's story and various mentions of her throughout the Gospels, it's time to connect this woman of the Bible with your own life. Fill out the chart below.

What do you see as Martha's greatest character strengths?	
What do you see as Martha's greatest character weaknesses?	
Which strengths do you relate to or long for?	
Which weaknesses do you relate to or long to overcome?	
How do you hope to be more like Martha in your faith journey?	

ℛEVEAL

Now that you've connected with this woman of the Bible, it's time to look at how Jesus reveals His character to Martha and how Jesus is doing the same for you.

Where did you most see Jesus show up in Martha's life and what does that reveal about God?	
What does Jesus reveal about Himself and His character in the life of Martha?	
Like Martha, in what ways have you experienced Jesus as the resurrection and the life?	
How is Jesus revealing Himself to you right now?	

$\mathcal{P}$RAY

Take a few minutes to ask the Holy Spirit to guide you as you respond to the following prayer prompts.

Lord, like Martha, help me . . .

_____

_____

_____

Lord, where am I out of balance in my service for You and enjoyment of You? What changes do I need to make to fully display my love in word and action toward You?

_____

_____

_____

Lord, where do You want to reveal Yourself as the resurrection and life in my life and relationships?

_____

_____

_____

Lord, how are You asking me to serve You now?

_____

_____

_____

Lord, considering Martha's story, how are You calling me to live differently?

_____

_____

_____

$\mathcal{P}$AIRS

We often look at women in the Bible on their own. By looking at them in pairs, according to their relationships and life situations, we can better understand ourselves, God, and others.

Mary of Bethany and her sister, Martha, are sometimes considered opposites. One of the most remarkable things about them is Jesus' close friendship with both, even though their personalities couldn't have been more different.

How does Jesus love, accept, and celebrate each woman in her uniqueness?

What does it reveal about Jesus that He offers deep friendship with such a wide range of people and personalities?

Name someone who expresses his or her love of Jesus very differently than you whom you've been tempted to look down on or judge.

How does Jesus' close ties with Mary and Martha tell us about the roles of women in His life, ministry, and the early church?

Mary, Mother of Jesus

All too often, Christians fall into the mistake of thinking that our journey will always be filled with delight. Mary knew better. The grief and sorrow and pain we experience in this life are real, and we aren't called to ignore or suppress them. Mary's life, grounded in prayer and patience, showed the early Christians that the only road to lasting joy was often through sorrow and prayerful waiting for God. There was no other road to the resurrection but through the cross, and Mary's life leads us directly there.

—**From** *The Women of the Bible Speak*, **page 186**

*I*n learning about Mary—the Mary of Bethlehem with the shepherds and the wise men and the baby Jesus—one good way to understand her is to look at whom she was not only at the beginning, but also at the end of this exhilarating and heartbreaking journey. It reminds us that as followers of Jesus we will all face the cross and die to our own desires.

REFLECT

The sudden appearance of an angel announcing to a peasant girl that she was going to give birth to the long-awaited Messiah must have been overwhelming. Yet Jesus' soon-to-be mother transitions from disbelief to faithful acceptance.

Read Luke 1:26–38. Which of the following emotions do you think Mary felt when she encountered the angel and heard the announcement? Circle all that apply.

Awe	Excitement	Loneliness	Fear
Stress	Frustration	Calm	Alarm
Boredom	Acceptance	Overwhelm	Hope

How would you have responded if placed in Mary's situation?

What does Mary's response in verse 38 reveal about her character and faith?

Read Luke 1:39–45. What role does Elizabeth play in encouraging and supporting Mary?

List three people who have played crucial roles in encouraging and supporting you in a time of uncertainty and waiting.

✿ _____

✿ _____

✿ _____

Which three people have you encouraged and supported during their time of uncertainty and waiting?

✿ _____

✿ _____

✿ _____

Do you know who is facing uncertainty and waiting for you to rally around now? What's stopping you?

Read Luke 1:46–55. What characteristics of God does Mary celebrate in her song of worship?

Which of these are most meaningful to you now? Why?

When you're in a season of waiting or uncertainty, how does focusing on the character of God strengthen you?

> From the earliest days of Jesus' arrival, Mary and Joseph were often on the run, first from Herod, the king, who was determined to snuff out Jesus' young life. This threat sent them to Egypt for escape and, later, led them to Nazareth. But along the way, Mary received holy confirmation of the greater plan.
>
> —From *The Women of the Bible Speak*, page 182

Read Luke 2:25–38. Who does God send to Mary and Joseph to deliver encouragement and confirmation?

What warning does Simeon provide in Luke 2:34?

Read Luke 2:41–51. How did Jesus' actions as a boy impact His mother, Mary?

How would you have responded?

Read John 2:1–10. What role does Mary play in Jesus' first miracle in the Gospel of John?

What does her response to Jesus reveal about her faith in her son?

Mary was there at the foot of the cross as Jesus endured horrific torture. To even try to imagine her grief is too much for most of us to bear. Her precious Son—heralded by angels, celebrated by prophets, and lauded as a brilliant scholar—died a public death, with her as a witness.

Read John 19:26–27. How does Jesus honor and care for His mother at His death?

What does it reveal about Jesus that even in His greatest agony, He was still thinking about His earthly mother?

The Bible does not record any words of Mary at the resurrection or even after the Ascension. But she remains, at the heart of the early Church, her prayers sustaining the apostles.

Read Acts 1:13–14. What does Mary's presence in the Upper Room after the resurrection reveal about her faith? Her love of Jesus? Her prayer life?

How was Mary's life shaped by promises waiting to be fulfilled?

How has your life been shaped by promises waiting to be fulfilled?

What role do devotion and prayer play in your waiting for God's promises to be fulfilled to you?

How does Mary's life demonstrate great patience and humility?

Where do you most need to grow in patience and humility?

CONNECT

Now that you've read and reflected on Mary, Mother of Jesus' story and various mentions of her throughout the Bible, it's time to connect this woman of the Bible with your own life. Fill out the chart below.

What do you see as Mary's greatest character strengths?	
What do you see as Mary's greatest character weaknesses?	
Which strengths do you relate to or long for?	
Which weaknesses do you relate to or long to overcome?	
How do you hope to be more like Mary in your faith journey?	

REVEAL

Now that you've connected with this woman of the Bible, it's time to look at how Jesus reveals His presence to Mary, mother of Jesus, and how God is doing the same for you.

When did you most see Jesus deepen Mary's faith?	
What does Jesus reveal about Himself and His character in the life of Mary?	
Like Mary, in what ways have you experienced the presence and power of Jesus?	
How is Jesus revealing Himself to you right now?	

$\mathcal{P}$RAY

Take a few minutes to ask the Holy Spirit to guide you as you respond to the following prayer prompts.

Lord, like Mary, mother of Jesus, help me . . .

_____

_____

Lord, what's the hard thing for which You're calling me to do or trust You?

_____

_____

Lord, in what area of my life do I most need to reflect on Your character and goodness?

_____

_____

Lord, what are You asking me to trust You with no matter what the outcome?

_____

_____

_____

Lord, considering the story of Mary, the mother of Jesus, how are You calling me to live differently?

_____

_____

_____

MARY MAGDALENE

*J*n all the Gospels, we learn of the devotion and dedication of the Mary who came from the fishing town of Magdala, "Mary the Magdalene." That she is mentioned in all four suggests she was an important part of Jesus' life and story . . . Jesus makes the point several times in His ministry that the one who has experienced the greatest forgiveness will love the most, and Mary appears to have loved Jesus with passionate devotion.

—**From** *The Women of the Bible Speak*, **page 188**

Mary Magdalene is often famed for being a woman out of whom had come seven demons (Luke 8:2). But this is only a blip in her story. Not only did Mary Magdalene use her resources to support Jesus and the disciples, but she's entrusted as the first witness to the miracle of the resurrection. She teaches us nothing in our past is a match for Jesus' calling to share the good news.

REFLECT

One of the challenges in the New Testament is that so many women share the name, Mary. Scholars say this list includes: Mary, the mother of Jesus; Mary of Bethany, sister of Martha; Mary, the mother of James and Joseph (Mark 15:40); Mary, the mother of John Mark (Acts 12:12); Mary of Clopas (identified as the sister-in-law); and Mary Magdalene.

Mary, from the fishing town of Magdala, is identified by her geographic home, as Mary Magdalene.

Read Luke 8:1–3. How is Mary Magdalene introduced in this passage?

What does this reveal about Mary Magdalene's character and the work of God in her life?

What's one thing in your past that Jesus has set you free from and redeemed?

How has Jesus' presence in your life affected the way you spend your money, time, and giftedness?

Read John 20:1–2. Why is it significant that a woman would be the first witness to the resurrection?

With whom does Mary Magdalene trust her discovery?

What does this suggest about Mary Magdalene's relationship with the disciples?

Read John 20:11–13. How do God's angels meet Mary Magdalene during her devastation and grief?

How has God met you in your moments of devastation and grief?

Read John 20:14–16. Describe a time when overwhelming grief made it difficult for you to recognize Jesus.

How did Jesus reveal Himself to you?

What's one word Jesus has or might speak to you that would bring you overwhelming joy?

Rabboni means not just "teacher," but "my teacher." And in this one word we see the foundations of Mary's relationship to Jesus. She acknowledged Him as a teacher and master, but this doesn't fully describe their bond. To admit that Jesus is the teacher is to see only part of the equation. He needs to be our teacher, one with whom we have a two-way relationship.

From *The Women of the Bible Speak*, pages 191–192

Read John 20:17. Are there any ways in which you're clinging to something old from Jesus when He wants to give you something new? If so, describe.

Read John 20:18. Which of the following best describes Mary Magdalene's response to Jesus? Place a check (√) by all that apply.

_____ Obedient   _____ Expectant   _____ Joyful   _____ Shy

_____ Faithful   _____ Hopeful   _____ Courageous   _____ Excited

When you share the good news of Jesus, which of these best describes your attitudes and words?

How can you share the good news of Jesus with others with the same exuberance?

CONNECT

Now that you've read and reflected on much of Mary Magdalene's story, it's time to connect this woman of the Bible with your own life. Fill out the chart below.

What do you see as Mary Magdalene's greatest character strengths?	
What do you see as Mary Magdalene's greatest character weaknesses?	
Which strengths do you relate to or long for?	
Which weaknesses do you relate to or long to overcome?	
How do you hope to be more like Mary Magdalene in your faith journey?	

REVEAL

Now that you've connected with this woman of the Bible, it's time to look at how Jesus reveals His never-ending love to Mary Magdalene and how Jesus is doing the same for you.

Where did you most see Jesus show up in Mary Magdalene's life?	
What does Jesus reveal about Himself and His character in the life of Mary Magdalene?	
Like Mary Magdalene, in what ways have you experienced a powerful encounter with Jesus?	
How is Jesus revealing Himself to you right now?	

$\mathcal{P}$RAY

Take a few minutes to ask the Holy Spirit to guide you as you respond to the following prayer prompts.

Lord, like Mary Magdalene, help me . . .

_____

_____

_____

Lord, with whom are You calling me to share the good news of Your resurrection this week?

_____

_____

_____

Lord, how can I share the good news of Your resurrection with joy and expectation like Mary Magdalene?

_____

_____

_____

Lord, what are You asking me to give up to support Your work in this world?

_____

_____

_____

Lord, considering Mary Magdalen's story, how are You calling me to live differently?

_____

_____

_____

$\mathcal{P}$AIRS

We often look at women in the Bible on their own. By looking at them in pairs, according to their relationships and life situations, we can better understand ourselves, God, and others.

These two Marys inhabited the same time and place, following Jesus in His earthly ministry. They likely knew each other and spent a great deal of time together. Though their stories differ wildly before the crucifixion, they come together afterward as those who refuse to desert Jesus. Their passionate devotion and love of Christ sew their stories together forever.

How have you experienced Mary, mother of Jesus, and Mary Magdalene as more than symbols and instead as real, living women through your study?

What would your life look like if you spent your days drinking in Christ's teaching, following His path, and living it out in the busyness of life?

How does each Mary's story demonstrate that the life of following Jesus will include conflict, sorrow, and grief alongside joy and hope?

How does that give you encouragement today?

JESUS AND THE WOMEN

Again and again, we see Jesus interacting with women who needed compassion, whether because of their own actions or because of circumstances beyond their control. He didn't shy away from sinners or women with no status. In fact, He walked right into their stories and into their lives in a way that not only offered them hope centuries ago, but also provide encouragement and inspiration for us today.

—**From** *The Women of the Bible Speak*, **page 200**

Throughout the Gospels, we encounter women who lived in the time of Christ who knew and interacted with Him, but whose names aren't mentioned. Yet all of them help us see, know, and believe in Jesus more.

REFLECT

In John 8, we meet an unnamed woman who is about to be killed for committing adultery. Yet rather than define her by her sin, she is freed by Jesus' forgiveness.

Read John 8:1–11. How does Jesus give this woman dignity and a second chance?

How has He done the same for you?

How has Jesus specifically and lovingly confronted your sin and redirected you toward lasting change?

In John 4, Jesus travels out of His way to visit and interact with a woman in Samaria. Though the religious leaders despised the region and people, Jesus made a beeline there to bring good news.

Read John 4:5–9. How does Jesus demonstrate there's no racism, classism, or sexism in the kingdom of God?

How have you shared Jesus with people right where they are, regardless of social norms?

Read John 4:10–13. How does Jesus address this marginalized woman?

Read John 4:14–18. What does Jesus' response to the Samaritan woman have in common with His response to the woman who committed adultery in John 8?

What does this reveal about the kindness with which God leads us to repentance (Romans 2:4)?

Read John 4:19–26 and John 4:39–41. The Samaritan woman led many to Jesus through her testimony that most certainly included the unsavory parts. When you share your testimony about Jesus with others, do you tend to include or exclude the unsavory parts?

How can sharing what Jesus has done and redeemed in the darkest parts of your life (in a healthy way) bring others to know Christ?

How does Jesus' interactions with these women reveal that salvation is a gift available to anyone no matter where they've been or what they've done?

Jesus also reaches out to women who are in dire straits because of where they find themselves in life, battered and bruised by their circumstances, and in deep need.

Read Luke 7:11–16. How does Jesus bring healing and hope to this devastated woman? What is the result?

> *his* woman had no husband, and had lost her only son—possibly the only person with a real opportunity to provide for her and watch over her. The image we see here is of a woman walking in her own son's funeral procession, crushed with grief and very likely worried about what will happen to her.
>
> From *The Women of the Bible Speak*, page 212

Read Mark 12:41–44. How does Jesus celebrate a woman who was invisible to everyone else?

What does this reveal about Jesus seeing you when you feel most invisible, unnoticed, or unappreciated?

Read Mark 1:29–31. How does Jesus reveal His power with Peter's mother-in-law?

What's her response?

What's your response to Jesus' healing power in your life?

Luke 13:10–13. Reflecting on this story, are there any wounds or injuries from the past that you believe are beyond Jesus' healing power?

How does this story challenge the limitations of your thinking?

Read Luke 8:40–56. What does Jesus do for the women in this passage physically, relationally, and spiritually?

When are you tempted to believe that God can only work in your life and not someone else's at the same time?

What encouragement and hope do you find in Jesus working in so many women's lives?

CONNECT

Now that you've read and reflected on several stories of unnamed women in the Gospels, it's time to connect Jesus' work with these women and your own. Fill out the chart below.

What happens to these women when they're willing to bring their sickness and weaknesses to Jesus?	
How does Jesus respond to these women who are honest and vulnerable with Him?	
What have you been holding back from Jesus for fear He'll reject you? How do these women challenge that belief?	
How do you hope to encounter the healing and restoration of Jesus like these women?	

REVEAL

Now that you've connected with these women of the Gospels, it's time to look at how Jesus reveals His character and faithfulness to you.

What does Jesus reveal about Himself and His character through these stories of healing and redemption?	
Like these women, what does Jesus require of you to encounter Him and His healing presence?	
Like these women, in what ways have you experienced a powerful encounter with Jesus?	
How is Jesus revealing Himself to you right now?	

$\mathscr{P}$RAY

Take a few minutes to ask the Holy Spirit to guide you as you respond to the following prayer prompts.

Lord, like these women you healed and restored, will You . . .

Lord, where have I been trying to encounter You on my terms rather than Your own? How can I trust You more?

Lord, where have I been holding back from You for fear of rejection or humiliation? How can I break free from those false beliefs?

Lord, which person can I help bring to You for Your healing and restoration?

Lord, considering these women's stories, how are You calling me to live differently?

ABOUT THE AUTHOR

Shannon Bream is the author of the #1 New York Times bestsellers *The Women of the Bible Speak* and *The Mothers and Daughters of the Bible Speak*, the anchor of *Fox News @ Night*, and the chief legal correspondent for Fox News Channel. She has covered landmark cases at the Supreme Court and heated political campaigns and policy battles from the White House to Capitol Hill.

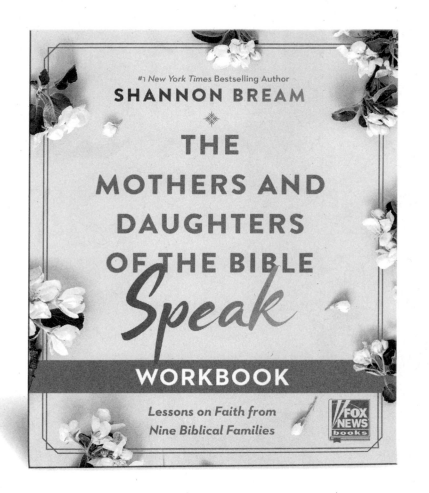